Leadership Condensed into Four Essentials

Paul Rocca

ISBN 9798864655108
Independently Published

Leadership Condensed into Four Essentials/Paul Rocca 2022 1st edition

I want to dedicate this book to the leaders who want to be more than just a person in charge and giving orders—someone who wants their team members to achieve their best and develop their organization. I am grateful for the organization called Teen Challenge, and it was one of the highlights of my life. I also want to thank my lifelong friends, Charl Johnson, Ruan Honiball, Dave Burgis, Troy Leggett, and Doug Coleman. I appreciate your friendships. I would especially like to thank my Uncle Dominic and Aunty Teresa. They have treated me like a son.

Contents

Introduction

For decades, I have enthusiastically studied leadership. I started my journey in leadership in my early twenties. I read books on the subject and then applied it as I supervised. I took notes as I learned from my own mistakes and successes.

I also learned from my colleagues and others in leadership. Eventually, after decades of being a student of many great authors and applying what I learned in my contracting business as well, I received what I believe to be a breakthrough. Four pillars for the requirements of leadership stood out to me, and I didn't get this from anyone else. For example, when I visited various worksites, I noticed some who were great in the skills of their profession but were not good at people skills. Others had good people skills but were not good at planning toward their goal/vision. Rarely will you find a leader operating powerfully in all four leadership essentials. I also noticed that many great books were devoted to people skills.

This book is short and straight to the point. Every pillar of leadership is explained. It's aimed at being a summary—the essence of leadership. I start by giving you a definition of leadership. Surprisingly, many leaders do not know the precise definition of leadership. Many think it's simply knowing your product/service better than anyone and holding a position of power while giving orders.

We will look at the different forms of training for knowing your product/service.

I will show you that it's the leader's responsibility to create an atmosphere where everyone can succeed. Also, great leaders will have a belief in their team. They are not afraid that their students or group will go further than them.

I will show you one study that proves contented people are 13% more productive.

I have chosen two world-famous leaders to study who were outstanding in leadership. I identify the four pillars of these leaders and show that using all of these pillars gives exceptional results. These world-famous leaders were high in emotional intelligence. I will provide you with a definition and show why having this quality is essential. For example, did you know that psychologists generally agree that IQ accounts for roughly 20% of the ingredients required for success? The rest depends on everything else—including emotional intelligence. (Emotional Quotient = E.Q. for short. A brief description of emotional intelligence is skill in perceiving, understanding, and managing emotions both in yourself and in others. I explain this further in chapter 6.)

I give you a historical example of high and low Emotional Intelligence in the situation of leadership.

We also look at vision and mission statements. I discuss the difference between the two. We will have a quick look at two current global corporations' vision and mission statements.

I will explain how to write your own mission and vision statement.

I will also show you bullying from the leadership of a company I visited on several occasions. Both work sites had the Emotional Intelligence skills of a drunken sailor! On both work sites, the projects went more than a year over the time budgeted!

We will also have a look at a comparison between tyrants and leaders. A journey to a long, far away destination requires careful planning. So too with a vision. We will have a good look at the essential elements of a plan of how to get to what your vision is. The leader must be focused on the vision and must continually progress towards that vision. This requires skill in planning and communication. This is done through staff meetings. Past performances are evaluated. Certain people who have achieved great results are recognized and honored. Also, meetings are discussed in detail, such as how often should you meet? Who is involved in the planning of the meeting? Can people miss important meetings? Can you meet too often? How can improvements be made in meetings? These questions will all be answered.

Definition of Leadership

Being in a position of leadership doesn't make you a leader. Many make the mistake of holding a position of power as leaders. Simon Sinek says it well, *"Leading is not the same as being the leader. Being the leader means you hold the highest rank, either by earning it, good fortune, or navigating internal politics. Leading, however, means that others willingly follow you—not because they have to, not because they are paid to, but because they want to."*[1]

Leadership is a combination of art and science. People skills are an art, and knowing your product or service is the science. There have been so many bestselling books written on leadership. So many great books have been written because people skills are an art, and this art can be learned. You will never stop learning people skills and about your product/service.

MANY GREAT PEOPLE HAVE TRIED TO DEFINE LEADERSHIP

Here are a few:

"Leadership is all about people. It is not about organizations. It is not about plans. It is not about strategies. It is all about people-motivating people to get the job done. You have to be people-centered."[2]

Coliln Powell

I like this definition because it includes the often-forgotten aspect of being people-centered. However, what is left out is it requires leading people toward a goal.

Daniel Goleman's definition:

> *"Leadership is not dominance, but the art of leading people to work towards a common goal."* [3]

This would have to be one of my favorites and the closest to my definition of leadership. This definition is accurate. However, I like to go beyond this definition because many issues can affect leadership—for example, loss of trust. The leader may motivate their team towards a goal, but if there is broken trust, it can be one of the hardest things to repair and seriously affect the performance of the individual or even the entire team.

> *"As we look ahead into the next century, leaders will be those who empower others."* [4]
>
> Bill Gates

The problem with this quote is there is no mention of mentoring a team or heading toward a vision.

> *"Leadership is the ability to inspire a team to achieve a certain goal."* [5]
>
> Tony Robbins

This is a brilliant quote. And close to my definition. I respect Tony as a popular leader. However, I take it further than influence because the best leaders in the past built relationships with their teams, as I will show you throughout my book.

Warren Bennis defines it like this:

"Leadership is the capacity to translate vision into reality." [6]

The problem with this quote is that it doesn't mention the process of building a team and mastering the knowledge of your product or service. It only states the vision and somehow getting there with an unknown ability.

Summary:

My Definition of Leadership:

My definition is simple and precise. I identify four pillars that are contained in good leadership. In this book, I show you that all the outstanding historical leaders I have included as examples have shown great people skills. One of the great books I read was "The Inspirational Leader" by Gifford Thomas. In this book, he devotes a whole chapter to this principle. He titles it, "Leadership Requires that You Build a Relationship with Your Team, Here's Why." (Chapter 2.) I thoroughly recommend this book.

One of my favorite quotes from this book is, *"If you have no relationship with your team and are comfortable with your people coming to work, completing their task, and leaving with no type of interaction, please, do us a favor and don't call yourself a leader."* [7]

We've looked at the attempted definitions of leadership, and I believe I have proven that leadership has more than one simple element. Here is mine: leadership is the art of building relationships as you head towards a goal. You will see two pillars within this statement:

1. **Mentoring** those whom you will lead through building a relationship.

2. **A vision/goal** that you are heading towards. From here, we go on to the other two essentials:

3. **A plan** on how to get there.

4. **Know your product/service**. You must know your product/service.

NOTES

_____

_____

_____

_____

_____

_____

_____

_____

_____

_____

_____

_____

_____

_____

_____

_____

_____

_____

_____

_____

_____

_____

_____

_____

_____

_____

_____

_____

_____

_____

_____

_____

_____

_____

_____

_____

_____

_____

_____

_____

_____

_____

_____

_____

_____

_____

_____

_____

_____

Examples of Great Leaders

SUN TZU "THE ART OF WAR"

Many believe that Sun Tzu was a Chinese general, military strategist, writer, and philosopher who lived in ancient China. His birth name was Sun Wu. The name Sun Tzu, by which he is commonly known, means Master Sun, a title of honor. He is most notably known for having written The Art of War, an influential work of military strategy.

The exact time and place of his birth are still a mystery, although most historians believe that Sun Tzu lived in an era called 'The Spring and Autumn Period of China,' dated between 770BC and 476BC. Sun Tzu, historians assume, was born in the city called Qi, in the Wu state of ancient China. Sun Tzu is believed to have been an ordinary soldier in the army of King He Lu of Wu. Some Chinese scholars around the 12th century AD began to doubt the historical existence of Sun Tzu, primarily because he is not mentioned in the nation's historical writings Zou Zhuang, which dates most of the notable figures from around 770 BC to 470 BC (the Spring and Autumn period.) It could therefore have been a collection of writings compiled into various generals' books. This seems to me to be the most viable theory.

Sun Tzu's "The Art of War" has influenced warfare strategies for more than two thousand years. It is believed to be one of the earliest forms of psychological warfare. It continues to be an influential piece of literature in modern warfare, politics, sports, and business. Apparently, although his troops were outnumbered ten to one in one conflict, he was still victorious.

Essential # 1 A vision/goal

We know little about Sun Tzu's vision/goals. I believe the evidence points to a collection of writings by various Generals, who had no long-term goals. Short-term goals were to win in battle.

Essential #2 A mentoring program

Sun Tzu's mentoring/team-building program was, without a doubt, one of the two strengths of his leadership. (The second was planning.) His quotes in this passage are eye-opening. He shows the benefits of building quality relationships within your organization.

"Treat your men as you would your own beloved sons. And they will follow you into the deepest valley."[1]

"When one treats people with benevolence, justice, and righteousness, and reposes confidence in them, the army will be united in mind, and all will be happy to serve their leaders."[2]

"If soldiers are punished before they have grown attached to you, they will not prove submissive; and, unless submissive, then will be practically useless. If, when the soldiers have become attached to you, punishments are not enforced, they will still be useless."[3]

These profound statements add to my argument that my definition of leadership is the art of building relationships as you head toward your goal/vision.

Essential # 3 Knowledge of your product/service

Sun Tzu's collection of war experiences is outstanding. Because he continually learned, he knew his service better than his rivals. Although we do not know his military equipment or the specific battles he had, his planning and team building are world-class and still used throughout the world.

Essential # 4 A plan of how to get there

Preparation was Sun Tzu's strength. To go into battle without preparation is suicidal. Same with your business. Whether planning to attack an enemy in war or competing with the opposition to your company, you must know your Strengths, Weaknesses, Opportunities, and Threats. Abbreviated as S.W.O.T. For Sun Tzu, it was Preparation! Preparation! Preparation! Combined with Team building, Team building! Team building! These quotes show this preparation:

"If you know the enemy and know yourself, you need not fear the result of a hundred battles. If you know yourself but not the enemy, for every victory gained, you will also suffer a defeat. If you know neither the enemy nor yourself, you will succumb in every battle." [4]

"Victorious warriors win first and then go to war, while defeated warriors go to war first and then seek to win." [5]

Thus, we may know that there are five essentials for victory:

1. *He will win who knows when to fight and when not to fight.*

2. *He will win who knows how to handle both superior and inferior forces.*

3. *He will win whose army is animated by the same spirit throughout*

all its ranks.

4. *He will win who, prepared himself, waits to take the enemy unprepared.*

5. *He will win who has military capacity and is not interfered with by the sovereign.* [6]

Here we have insight into his team building:

"A leader leads by example, not by force." [7] What a great insight into leadership! When you must resort to force in leadership, you are supposing that the person to whom you are directing doesn't want to be there, as well as abusing the power of your position and creating mistrust. This is a situation you would never want. When you have people in your organization who don't want to be there, you show that people are unwilling to follow you in heading toward your intended goal. Using force should be your absolute last resort! You don't need to threaten self-motivated people who believe in a common goal.

It is highly likely that the great leader Field Marshal Erwin Rommel adapted this quote and expanded on it into his famous words: *"Be an example to your men, in your duty, and in private life. Never spare yourself and let the troops see that you don't in your endurance of fatigue and privation. Always be tactful and well-mannered and teach your subordinates to do the same. Avoid excessive sharpness or harshness of voice, which usually indicates the man who has shortcomings of his own to hide."* [8]

As I said before, here is another great insight into Sun Tzu's relationship expertise with his team: *"Regard your soldiers as your children, and they will follow you into the deepest valleys; look on them as your own beloved sons, and they will stand by you even unto death."* [9]

Once more, it is highly likely that Erwin Rommel was captivated by this quote and reworded it into his liking: *"Winning the men's confidence requires much of a commander. He must exercise care and caution, look after his men, live under the same hardships, and, above all, apply self-discipline. But once he has their confidence, his men will follow him through hell and high water."* [10]

Summary of Sun Tzu's Leadership:

Sun Tzu knew his product/service (war) well and the team he led. He not only knew his product/service very well, but he built strong relationships to inspire people towards his goal. He combined the art of relationships and the science of warfare flawlessly. History has not recorded any of his military conflicts, but his essential planning of how to get there and his mentoring program were world-class.

ALEXANDER THE GREAT

Alexander the Great, also known as Alexander III or Alexander of Macedonia, is considered one of the most outstanding military leaders in all history.

Alexander was born in Pella, Macedonia in 356 B.C. His father was King Philip II. Alexander was taught to read, write, and play the lyre as a young boy. His father hired the famous Aristotle to be his private teacher. He studied with Aristotle for three years, and from Aristotle's teachings, Alexander developed a love of science, particularly medicine and botany. Alexander included botanists and scientists in his army to study his conquered lands.

A political rival assassinated his father at the age of 20. Alexander became king of Macedonia. Alexander began his reign by subduing opponents in the Greek and Macedonian regions. Alexander started his invasion of the Middle East in 334 B.C.

In thirteen short years, he went on to conquer the Middle East, all the way to the shore of the Ganges River of India and Egypt. He was undefeated in battle. Military Academies still use his tactics today.

Alexander was 32 when he died in 323 B.C.

Alexander's leadership measured against the Four Essentials:

Essential # 1 A vision/goal

Get your team united with one goal in mind.

To be free from the tyrannical rule of the Persians. He was unsurpassed in conquering so much in so little time, except for Genghis Khan. By the time he reached the Ganges River in India, his army was exhausted and homesick. They refused to follow him any further. His vision was massive! Look at this famous quote just before his death in Babylon: *"There are no more worlds to conquer!"* [11] This reveals the power of his single-minded focus on the goal in his mind.

Alexander kept his vision in front of himself constantly. Not only was his vision of what he wanted to conquer–the then-known world, but he also held a picture of who he wanted to be like—Achilles. He kept a unique copy of the Iliad beneath his pillow wherever he slept. Every leader needs a mentor.

Alexander made it clear as he sold his vision that he and his army were fighting for something greater than wealth and power–eternal glory. He kept an idea of who he wanted to be like—Achilles, the hero who valued his legacy above all else. When Achilles was born, he was given a prophecy that he would either live a peaceful, long life in obscurity or a short life but achieve eternal glory.

After Achilles' best friend, Patroclus, was killed, he returned to battle and got revenge. According to the story, he dies shortly after killing Homer and hundreds of other Trojan soldiers. Achilles lived a short life but achieved eternal glory. Above all, this is what Alexander wanted.

Essential # 2 A Mentoring Program

Without a doubt, Alexander's leadership was attributed to the personal tutoring by one of the best philosophers of the time, Aristotle. Think about this: philosophy greatly helps with people skills. This allowed him to translate his vision of where he wanted to be through building relationships with his team. He was an example to his men and held up others as examples.

When Alexander rose to power, it looked impossible to unite his fractured homeland of the Macedonians and the Greeks. They had been at war for centuries. The rivalry between the Macedonians and the Athenians or Greeks separated them into two camps. The Macedonians were considered barbarians by the Athenians, and the Macedonians were viewed as monarchical and tribal. The Athenians were thought to be highly democratic and highly cultured. They looked down upon the Macedonians as of a lower class. On the other hand, the Macedonians considered the Greeks to be inferior fighters.

It looked impossible to have a united group with the same focus to achieve his goals. But two things worked in his favor: 1) A familiar shared mythology and 2) A desire for freedom from slavery from the Persians, which will be discussed in essential 4. They were all familiar with the story of Homer and other myths. These ancient heroes gave them something in common to focus on and brought team unity.

Alexander also mentored them with the current top-selling book of the day–The Iliad. He inspired them in a new Trojan war that they were all familiar with, but this time it was the Persians in place of the people of Troy.

He led his army to the ruins of Troy at the outset of his campaign into Asia and honored the heroes who died there. When the opportunity presented itself, he reminded his team of the book they were studying—their common admiration of their past heroes in the Iliad. This built team unity. No longer were they quarreling over minor issues.

Like the Greeks, who invaded Troy hundreds of years before, Alexander's army sought revenge against a brutal eastern power. Alexander cast their march into Asia as a new Trojan War.

He invoked this common past every chance he got through public sacrifices to the gods and the heroes his soldiers admired. Instead of a diverse group of people bickering over petty grudges, they were a united Greek army seeking the same success as their shared ancestors. His focus and drive were for the advancement of his team.

Through his words, behavior, and lifestyle, Alexander painstakingly made the case that he was fighting for the glory and honor of the army, not his enrichment. Alexander had great mentors, Aristotle, in his younger years, and Achilles, the greatest warrior in his favorite book, the Iliad. According to some sources on Alexander's life, he may have had a sense of rivalry against his hero. He firmly believed he was a direct descendant of him. This may have given him the confidence to accomplish great exploits.

When he led his army through the ruins of Troy, Alexander made a remarkable show of honoring Achilles at his tomb. *"I would rather see the lyre of Achilles, which he used to sing the glories of brave men,"* [12]

Essential # 3 Knowledge of his product/service

Alexander's service/product was war, which he knew very well. Even though heavily outnumbered, he was undefeated in battle, and Persia was the world's superpower then. As I said earlier, his battle tactics are still used in the military today.

Essential # 4 A plan of how to get there

The Greeks were slaves to the Persians, but the Greek states were fractured by in-fighting. One of the first things Alexander did was quell division and promote unity. Without this universal agreement, there could be no shared vision. He appealed to them with this quote: *"Youths of the Pellaians and of the Macedonians and of the Hellenic Amphictiony and of the Lakedaimonians and of the Corinthians... and of all the Hellenic peoples, join your fellow soldiers and entrust yourselves to me so that we can move against the barbarians and liberate ourselves from the Persian bondage, for as Greeks we should not be slaves to barbarians."*[13] What must be considered part of Alexander's success is the people's desire for freedom. It's good to keep in mind a quote from C. S Lewis: *"Hardships often prepare ordinary people for an extraordinary destiny."*[14]

People look to a leader in a time of distress. Never underestimate a society with its backs to the wall! Learn to discern your team's dreams and desires. Appeal to them for mutual benefit and reap the benefits of a mutually shared goal!

Famous Inspirational quotes:

"We of Macedon for generations past have been trained in the hard school of danger and war."[15]

"Holy shadows of the dead, I'm not to blame for your cruel and bitter fate, but the accursed rivalry which brought sister nations and brother people to

fight one another. I do not feel happy for this victory of mine. On the contrary, I would be glad, brothers, if I had all of you standing here next to me, since we are united by the same language, the same blood, and the same visions." 16

"Are there no more worlds that I might conquer?"[17]

"Are you still to learn that the end and perfection of our victories is to avoid the vices and infirmities of those whom we subdue?" [18]

"I had rather excel others in the knowledge of what is excellent, than in the extent of my power and dominion." [19]

"With the right attitude, self-imposed limitations vanish." [20]

Summary of Alexander the Great's Leadership

Sometimes the perfect opportunity presents itself. For example, a people longing to be free from slavery. If the Greeks and Macedonians weren't so hungry for freedom, the Greek empire might never have happened.

Alexander was an outstanding leader who knew how to sell his vision and lived as one of the team. His vision was tremendous! He wanted to conquer the then-known world. He believed in his team and convinced the people that they could do it. He gave them courage by reminding them of their ancestor's exploits through the Iliad.

Undefeated in battle, he knew his product/service thoroughly. He routinely singled people out for honor and recognition. He recalled acts of bravery performed by former and fallen heroes, making it clear that each person, as far as possible, would be recognized and valued.

He mentored his team with his leadership technique, He led his troops literally from the front. When his troops went hungry or thirsty, he went hungry and thirsty. When their horses died beneath them, and they had to walk, he did the same.

This pattern of leadership only changed when he gave in to the luxury of Persian court life, and he was far removed from his people's sufferings.

1. He mentored his team by pointing them to who they would become, heroes, through the familiar writings of the Iliad.

2. He gave them a vision—to conquer the Persians and the known world,

3. He knew his product—strategy in warfare

4. And a plan of how to get there; one city at a time.

However, towards the end of his life, and particularly after the death of Hephaestion (one of his generals), Alexander started to show signs of megalomania. This most likely would have come through his outstanding achievements, combined with the consequences of continually thinking of himself as a god (after the style of Achilles). Additionally, his friends' flattery, all combined to provide this effect.

So, the lesson is, it doesn't matter how well you start. Think about finishing well too. The advice of good colleagues who will tell you what you do not want to hear is important. Remember that you're not above the people you serve.

NOTES

_____

_____

_____

_____

_____

_____

_____

_____

_____

_____

_____

_____

_____

_____

_____

_____

_____

_____

_____

_____

_____

_____

_____

_____

_____

_____

_____

_____

_____

_____

_____

_____

Essential One—A Goal/Vision

INTRODUCTION

Remember, our definition of leadership is building relationships toward a goal. In this chapter, we are going to study vision and mission statements. As a leader, you must have a clear definition of where you are guiding your team towards. A leader is the one who has the vision and articulates it into a statement so that other people can understand and follow it.

Once again, the brilliant innovator and visionary Steve Jobs confirms this concept: *"The greatest people are self-managing—they don't need to be managed. Once they know what to do, they'll go figure out how to do it. What they need is a common vision. And that's what leadership is: having a vision; being able to articulate that so the people around you can understand it and getting a consensus on a common vision."* [1]

A vision statement is vital to any organization because, without it, the organization is at risk of wandering aimlessly. It keeps all people on track and informs potential customers of what the corporation/service has to offer.

A vision statement is a direction of where your organization is heading. Therefore, it should describe accurately where you're heading, and it should be achievable.

Along with a vision statement is a mission statement that explains the organization's values and what it does in the day-to-day activities on the way to its destination. We will look at this distinction in further detail with an example from a business.

After this, we will study the vision and mission statements of two global corporations and observe the differences between the vision and mission statements.

Next, we look at writing both a vision and mission statement for those who may be starting a new enterprise. For all others, you may still look at this because it could help bring further clarity to this topic.

What's the Difference Between a Mission Statement and a Vision Statement?

Many people often ask this question. One of the differences between a mission statement and a vision statement is the present situation vs. the long-term future. The distinctions between the two are also about belongings/tangibles instead of thoughts or values. Your mission is what you offer right now, how you're making the goods or service available, where you conduct your service or sell, and an outline of how you're unique from the rest. Mission statements relate to doing, so they relate to your everyday operations. Your mission statement outlines the day-to-day things you will do to obtain your vision statement.

Here's an example from a flower shop to reveal the distinction between mission and vision. Fiona's flower shop aims to provide our customers with quality flowers and floral arrangements at a fair price.

Notice the present in this sentence. (Mission Statement) Fiona's Flower Shop will strive to become the leader in providing floral products and services in our country. We will always endeavor to maintain a tradition of exceeding customers' expectations at a reasonable price. (Vision Statement) Do you notice the future elements in the vision statement? Vision statements relate to seeing and planning, so they are about looking ahead. Your vision statement outlines your business ambitions and where you're headed.

DEFINITION OF A MISSION STATEMENT

A mission statement defines the existing condition of any business or company in one or two sentences. A mission statement resolves a minimum of three key questions:

What do we do?

Who do we do it for?

How do we do it differently or better?

When planning a mission statement, think about why the entity exists. Use words that will help someone quickly understand what you provide and the reason for the service or product.

Any entity that attempts to operate without a mission statement runs the risk of wandering without direction and not having the ability to verify that the organization is on its intended course.

DEFINITION OF A VISION STATEMENT

A vision statement is the direction your organization is headed. Therefore, it should describe accurately where you're headed, and it should be achievable. A vision statement is a sentence or two that expands on the mission statement by expressing values, visions, or dreams as they relate both internally and externally to the mission. Think about the values and the desired future destiny. What do you want the business/service to achieve? What is the "guiding star" for this enterprise that will not change even if leadership changes?

Your vision statement should be specific and stimulating to your staff and customers.

The words often seen in vision statements are achieve, believe, treat, etc. Descriptive words assist staff and clients in understanding what to expect.

For example, a vision statement may address "diversity of thought," as a value statement. This same mission statement mentions that all are responsible for customer and client assurances. Those phrases form a directive or demand for action by personnel. We often see a blending of vision and mission statements because if you hold values (consisting of high moral standards), those values compel you to take specific directives, e.g., satisfy customer guarantees.

When contemplating the distinction between mission statements and vision statements, these succinct definitions may help.

- **Vision statement** motives for now and future expectations.

- **Mission statement** primary activities and tangible targets today.

- **Statement of purpose** why the entity does what it does.

- **Values statement**, what is going to guide the organization's behaviors and beliefs.

There is not a great deal of distinction between mission and vision for some, but creating them as separate, specific statements will help make your thought process clearer and result in more successful results. If you can divide a topic, you will create greater understanding and so you will multiply your insight.

Coca-Cola's Vision and Mission Statement

Our Mission

Our Roadmap starts with our mission, which is enduring. It declares our purpose as a company and serves as the standard against which we weigh our actions and decisions.

- *To refresh the world...*

- *To inspire moments of optimism and happiness...*

- *To create value and make a difference.*

Our Vision

Our vision serves as the framework for our Roadmap and guides every aspect of our business by describing what we need to accomplish in order to continue achieving sustainable, quality growth.

- *People: Be a great place to work where people are inspired to be the best they can be.*

- *Portfolio: Bring to the world a portfolio of quality beverage brands that anticipate and satisfy people's desires and needs.*

- *Partners: Nurture a winning network of customers and suppliers, together we create mutual, enduring value.*

- *Planet: Be a responsible citizen that makes a difference by helping build and support sustainable communities.*

- *Profit: Maximize long-term return to share owners while being mindful of our overall responsibilities.*

- *Productivity: Be a highly effective, lean, and fast-moving organization."*[2]

Coca Cola. Mission and Vision Statement.

GENERAL MOTORS MISSION AND VISION STATEMENT

Their Mission Statement is *"to earn customers for life by building brands that inspire passion and loyalty through not only breakthrough technologies but also by serving and improving the communities in which we live and work around the world.'*

Their Vision Statement is *"to create a future of zero crashes, zero emissions, and zero congestion, and we have committed ourselves to leading the way toward this future."*[3]

General Motors Mission and Vision Statement Analysis.

Notice the differences between the mission statement and the vision statements? For Coca-Cola, its mission statement declares the purpose; *"Our Roadmap starts with our mission, which is enduring. It declares "as a company and serves as the standard against which we weigh our actions and decisions."* The mission is what they're doing in the present. It's their core value. This is what they live by, now. Notice in General Motors Mission Statement *"by serving and improving the communities in which we live and work around the world,"* it describes the organization's purpose for existing. This statement informs all the organization's actions—if an activity doesn't fit in with the mission statement, it should be dropped because it doesn't advance the organization toward its goals. The mission statement is an action-oriented statement declaring an organization's purpose to its audience. It often includes a general description of the organization, function, and objectives. As a company grows, its goals may be reached and change. Because of this, revise mission statements as needed to reflect the business's new culture as you meet previous goals.

Their vision statement relates to what is in their future. It refers to the direction and where they want to be. It requires looking toward where you want the organization to be. The vision statement looks forward to the future and works towards arriving at that goal one day. Notice General Motors vision *"to create a future of zero crashes, zero emissions, and zero congestion, and we have committed ourselves to leading the way toward this future."*

How to Write a Mission Statement

Ask yourself why you are in your chosen service/business.

This is the central question that will determine the nature and content of your mission statement. Also, ask yourself these questions:

- Why did you begin this enterprise?

- What are you aiming for? Decide what the specific reason for your entity. This is a way to get the thinking started. Here are some questions you could begin asking yourself:

- Who are your customers or the target audience you're trying to help?

- What role do you play within the organization?

Work out what makes your entity different from the rest.

The tone of your mission statement must replicate your enterprise's style and subculture—its character. Consider how your customers and other agencies find you and write down the traits you think may characterize your service/company. Observe the following questions:

- Do you need to be visible as an organization with a little humor and a playful side, or does it need to be formal?

- What's your company culture? Is there a strict dress code and a formality to the place, or are they allowed to come to work in casual clothes?

Determine what makes your service/sales points different from the rest. The core aim of your mission statement is to express your values. Whatever unique thing you are doing with your commercial enterprise, you should clearly define that in your message.

Make a list of your company's specific goals

Finally, your mission statement should include one or more tangible goals.

- What are your short-term plans?

- What's the highest objective that you are trying to obtain?

Your goals are to be centered around customer service, dominating a specific market, helping improve people's lives with your product, and so on.

Remember your service/company's character when writing down your goals. The two should reflect one another.

Designing The Statement

Outline your plans through actionable goals. Now that you've brainstormed a range of ideas, it is time to trim them down to the essential and most direct to get to the heart of your organization and what it has to offer. Write a sentence that captures what your organization is and what it determines to do.

Add concrete, quantifiable elements

Don't write a mission statement with a big, romantic vision that isn't rooted in anything definite. Mission statements that sound like they were copied and pasted from a mission statement generator cause people to lose interest and walk away.

Instead of saying something like "We aim to make the world a better place," mention which specific section of the market you're aiming to reach. Look back at your brainstorming notes for particular ideas.

Instead of saying something general like: we'll continue to develop our product to the best it can be, say something specific about what you are aiming to do. For example, we endeavor to make our hamburgers tastier than the others.

Add your touch

Use your wording so that it reflects your enterprise's personality and fashion. Your language should be formulated for your entity if it's formal and conservative. If it is playful and fun, you could get creative with the language to emphasize that side of your corporation. Check your brainstorming notes for ideas.

Word selection is important, but the general impression of your mission statement can also help you make a point. A few businesses begin with one phrase that completely encapsulates the essence of the corporation. Then they write a sentence or two expanding on it.

Often, it helps to break it down into smaller mission statements. How does your mission relate to your product?

Leave Out the Non-Essentials

A message with too many descriptive words can become meaningless. "As a collective team, we purpose to synergistically personalize software design, the futuristic tools of empowerment." This is an exaggeration, I know, but can you see how the message is lost? As you write your mission statement, cautiously choose phrases that mean something to you and your enterprise. Remember, a mission statement's point is to convey your organization's core values. Write what you and the average person would understand!

Don't Make it Too Long

Your mission statement must be clear, straight to the point, and usually no longer than a brief paragraph. This makes it easier to copy and showcase for the world to grasp. Do not go into too much detail in your statement that you struggle to describe it when asked. The ideal situation is that your mission statement becomes your slogan.

Get Other People You Trust Involved

If you're starting from nothing, search for someone who is successful in business or in the service industry. Go to them prepared with a list of ideas of what you like to achieve. Listen to them for constructive criticism. Very often, people can see things that you don't see. Write all their ideas down, even the ones you may not agree with. Think about them for a while. Sometimes one idea can be improved on. Or it may lead you to other ideas.

Once you have it completed, have someone proofread it for spelling and grammatical errors.

Test It Out

Put your mission statement on your internet site, print it on brochures, and find creative ways to get your message out aiming at those who are interested. What reactions do you receive? If you like the reaction you are getting, your message is serving its function. If it seems to confuse your target customers, you may need to rework it.

A good mission statement should lead your audience to confirm that their needs are being met.

HOW TO WRITE A VISION STATEMENT

Writing a good vision statement takes time. It only needs to be only a sentence or two in length. But each concept stated matters. Once you have your vision statement, it will not get adjusted until your entity grows out of it. So, you should be confident enough to back it 100%.

As you start working on your vision statement, here are some major facts to remember:

Start with thinking about your organization's main reason for being and its place in the market. Consider reading through your business plan a few times. This allows you to anchor your vision in the service/sales operations and your future direction.

Ask yourself what your sales/service entity does. Also, who is your target market? How does it assist your target market in getting what they want or need? What is it you're specifically looking to accomplish?

Think about what makes your organization special. It's vital to have a completely unique value proposal. You do not want your vision statement to sound vague.

You don't need to say how you'll go about obtaining your vision. You do not want to get lost in the details of logistics and plans in a vision statement. Simply need to define the ultimate intention you're striving for.

Make certain you are specific in your vision. Make sure that your goals are realistic and achievable. Don't use slang and do not use vague language. The average person should be able to understand it. Industry jargon will lose a lot of people. Consider the general public and their concerns.

Establish your statement in everyday language so readers can obtain a specific concept of your vision. This association can create an emotional bond. For example, I recall a time eating a hamburger at Hungry Jacks (Burger King in many other places.) My brother said to me, "The burgers are better at Hungry Jacks." He repeated their advertising slogan.

Ensure your values are accounted for. Your vision statement should fit seamlessly with the values of your organization. If there are contradictions, you will need to rework your statement.

CONCLUSION

My definition of leadership–which is building relationships toward a goal that is clearly understood. Therefore, it is essential to have your goal articulated and written down in a simple, easy-to-understand way. This way, others can grasp the vision and run beside you with your leadership. We have investigated the distinction between a vision and a mission statement, which has broadened our understanding of this area. We looked at two global corporations' vision and mission statements, which brought further clarity.

NOTES

_____

_____

_____

_____

_____

_____

_____

_____

_____

_____

_____

_____

_____

_____

_____

_____

_____

_____

_____

_____

_____

_____

_____

_____

_____

_____

_____

_____

_____

_____

_____

_____

_____

_____

_____

_____

_____

_____

_____

_____

_____

_____

_____

_____

_____

_____

Essential Two–Know Their Product/Service

INTRODUCTION

In an age of fierce competition amongst rivals, developing skills is vital for survival. You need to know that your product/service will give you an edge over the competition. A good leader knows what his or her team is capable of.

Add up the combined skills in each department. How much collective experience does your organization have? How well are they sharing that knowledge amongst themselves?

The speed at which your company grows will determine the need for hiring employees. There may not be enough time to grow your talent from your existing employees. This is where recruiting comes in. It is a cost-effective way to boost the skills of your team. We will briefly look at the latest developments in this process.

After this, we look at on-the-job training which is probably one of the oldest methods of skill development. Next, we will look at job rotation, where a person spends a specified time in each area of expertise. The aim is to give an overview of the corporate entity. Following this, we will look at the apprenticeship model. It is also one of the oldest methods of skill development. It is a style of learning that combines theoretical knowledge with practical hands-on skills. After this, we will look at coaching and mentoring. Although similar, there are distinctions, so we break them down, examine them, and give them a brief overview. Next, we will look at vestibule learning. This is a replicated workplace where the trainee is taught the necessary skills in the safety of a simulated environment. We will discuss the pros and cons.

Finally, we will discuss e-learning. This style of learning has multiplied. We discuss the advantages and disadvantages.

You can grow the collective skills within your organization in two ways:

RECRUIT PEOPLE WHO ARE ALREADY EXPERTS IN THIS AREA

There will be many times when you must hire new people, rather than train someone within your organization. Steve Jobs said it well, *"We hired truly great people and gave them the room to do great work. A lot of companies [...] hire people to tell them what to do. We hire people to tell us what to do. We figure we're paying them all this money; their job is to figure out what to do and tell us."* [1]

An Example of a Recruitment Process

Selecting employees for unskilled labor is relatively easy and low risk. Just look at resumes, references, etc., and take a chance to see if they are what they say on their resumes. If things don't work out, move them on and hire another. This is not so easy when you move further up in skill requirements. Recruiting high-caliber candidates can be difficult. Gone are the days when companies relied on degrees, certificates, or resumes.

Sometimes companies run through a process to find the right person. Here is an example of one person's approach, Elon Musk. Elon's interview procedures are unique to the man himself. They question the candidates and fully test their intelligence. This often involves candidates submitting their CVs (curriculum vitae or resume) and taking telephone interviews with employers. The best-qualified people will receive interviews with a team of employees. Interview questions and tests with Elon Musk companies are very long. One prospective employee reportedly had to endure a coding test for 6 hours with his test procedure.

The pressure starts abruptly when candidates are forced to tolerate marathon negotiations with many examiners. These examiners ask specific questions about their previous knowledge to measure the depth of their knowledge. Candidates will be provided with a simulated environment that has problems to solve.

If the candidates go through this phase, they will have to go through an interview with Elon Musk himself. Musk will interview the person and ask specific questions about their roles in the three special projects he has worked on. He will ask these questions to determine the depth of knowledge and involvement the candidate has played in previous special assignments. Musk will also look for a positive attitude towards the candidates.

Using Employees to Help Find New Talent

According to the 2018 Growth Hiring Trends and research in the US, more than 67% of the fastest-growing companies are on the list of discovering and creating new talent pools with the help and ideas of current employees.[2] Not much has changed, according to Elon Musk, who added, *"Anyone at Tesla can, and should, email/talk to anyone else according to what they think is the fastest way to solve a problem for the benefit of the whole company."*[3]

TRAIN PEOPLE UP IN YOUR EXISTING TEAM

Teaching Style # 1. On-The-Job-Training

On-the-job training (OJT) is obtained through work experience, and so it is frequently called "on-the-job" training. The essence of OJT is to use the existing people, surroundings, tools, and talent training available within the place of employment to train employees to do their jobs—at the place of employment. It's commonly used to teach employees a way to do their contemporary jobs. The employee learns to master their skills under the supervision of their trainer.

Usually, no new tools or area is needed. The trainee is being trained on the premises where everything is available. The teacher may be a specialist or a tradesperson. The skilled person simply teaches the unskilled person through supervision until they have mastered their skill.

On-the-job training consists of several steps. First, the trainee receives an overview of the job, its purpose, and its desired outcomes, with an emphasis on the relevance of the training. Then the teacher demonstrates the task to give the personnel a model to copy. Since the employee is demonstrated the skills that the activity calls for, the training is transferable to the task.

Next, the worker is allowed to copy the instructor's example. Demonstrations through the trainer and exercises by the trainee are repeated until the process is mastered. Repeated demonstrations and practice provide repetition and feedback. Eventually, the employee does the task without supervision, although the teacher might also go to the worker to see if there are any lingering questions.

This form of training has many benefits. It is easy to set up. It's practical. It encourages self-mastery. It speeds up the worker's adjustment to his trainer and fellow workers and can be very cost-effective.

This technique enables efficient transfer in terms of mastering concepts because schooling and actual work conditions are nearly identical. It gives practical experience, and it's easy to see the results.

This method does have its disadvantages. The assigned teacher can be poor. He can be easily distracted by the pressures of work or other things. In their desire for immediate production, the trainee may fail to examine the most efficient way of doing the task. The actual costs the lost time of trainee and trainer, as well as wasted resources and damaged tools, may not be cost-effective.

It is usually short and poorly structured. Additionally, many established employees may resent coaching an unskilled colleague, and the incapable employee can be pressured to master the skills before they're competent.

Before implementing on-the-job training programs, one should consider certain things:

- The selection of teachers should be primarily based on their ability to teach and their desire to do so.

- The trainers should be aware of the correct techniques to demonstrate.

- The trainer's progress should frequently be assessed then, and the trainee should be assessed using reliable measurements.

- Mentors and trainees should be cautiously paired so that you can reduce differences in language, personality, attitudes, or age that could inhibit conversation.

- The teacher must be made to realize the significance of near supervision so one can keep away from trainee accidents.

- On-the-job training (OJT) should be used alongside other training strategies and programmed education, lectures, and videos.

Teaching Style # 2. Job Rotation

To cross-train employees in various jobs, some trainers move a trainee from job to job. Each move is typically preceded by job instruction training. This is a training method where workers rotate through various jobs, thereby giving them more experience. Trainees are placed in different jobs in different parts of the organization for a specified time.

They may spend several days or even years in different company locations. In this way, they get an overall perspective of the organization. Besides giving workers variety in their jobs, it helps the organization with vacations, if they happen to downsize, or if resignations occur. It helps workers sharpen their career objectives and develops people for higher-level positions by exposing them to a wide range of experience in a relatively short span of time.

Both blue-collar production workers and white-collar managers use this, and it has many organizational benefits. Learner participation and high job transferability are the learning advantages of job rotation. Job rotation creates flexibility. During workforce shortages, workers have the skills to step in and fill open positions.

The method also provides new and different work on a systematic basis, giving employees a variety of experiences and challenges. Employees also increase their flexibility and marketability because they can perform various tasks.

However, this method also has its limitations. The major drawback is that it is time-consuming and expensive too. This method can be effective when the trainees are placed in company locations where they receive maximum feedback, reinforcement, and performance monitoring by competent, responsible, and experienced trainers.

Due to individual differences, people are not equally suited for all jobs. It weakens a worker's commitment to a given job. Job rotation also challenges one of the basic principles of personnel placement–that workers be assigned jobs that best match their talents and interests.

Teaching Style # 3. Apprenticeship

Apprenticeship schooling is one of the oldest methods of training. Students receive a regular fixed income for services to learn their trade. It combines practical experience with theoretical knowledge. An apprentice is an employee who is getting to know a trade but has not reached the point wherein he is ready to work without supervision. It is incredibly commonplace inside the skilled trades. Employers use trained tradesmen/tradeswomen, including carpenters, plumbers, masons, printers, and sheet metal employees may also develop tradespeople through apprenticeships.

An unskilled employee is "tutored" by a skilled worker for an extended period. An apprenticeship lasts from two to 5 years. In addition to on-the-job training, trainees are also required to learn in a classroom environment. Different trades require different amounts of classroom activity. Each apprentice is typically given a workbook, which includes analyzing materials, assessments to be taken, and practical theory problem-solving.

The apprentice serves as an assistant and learns the craft by operating with a fully skilled member of the trade referred to as a tradesman. This education is used in such trades, crafts, and technical fields wherein talent may be obtained after a relatively long period of time in direct affiliation with the work and underneath the direct supervision of specialists. In the apprenticeship program, they are known as an apprentice. When the man or woman graduates, they officially graduate into a tradesman or tradeswoman.

Apprenticeship schooling has been criticized by some industry experts that the training programs essentially discriminate and give preferential treatment to family and friends.

One of the most significant disadvantages for the trainee/apprentice is the time inside the program regardless of the skills learned. This results in a few skilled apprentices remaining at low wages, a scenario agencies have exploited on occasion. The amount of time an apprenticeship lasts is predetermined, usually by trade governing bodies.

Next, we look at two similar other types of skills development: Coaching and Mentoring.

One of the most common questions people ask is "what is the difference between mentoring and coaching?"

Coaches develop talents in people or corporations, offer guidance and vision, and offer training, sources, and advice on skills to enhance their performance. Coaching centers on the specific project and overall performance evaluation based on the review. Coaches give targets for the learner and continuously measure performance over the years.

Mentoring has similarities with coaching, but with some differences. A mentor is a more experienced man or woman with a desire to impart knowledge to a person less skilled in a relationship. This must be done in an arrangement of mutual respect.

Like coaches, mentors provide direction and encouragement, but focus on the mentee on a specific potential or ability. Mentors approach the training of their mentees holistically and consider what drives them and what situations they might face in the direction of their commonly agreed-upon ambitions.

In addition to providing input and instruction on ability and improvement, mentors assist their mentees in learning their organization's culture, provide support to instill attitudes and values to advance the mentees through teachable moments and provide possibilities for them to develop through self-discovery.

Teaching Style # 4. Coaching

At the management level, teaching trainees by using their managers is another method. Education is just like apprenticeships because the coach attempts to provide a version for the trainee to copy. It tends to be much less formal than an apprenticeship program because there are few formal classroom sessions.

Coaching is sort of always treated by way of the supervisor or manager, not through the HR department. Participation and interaction are likely to be excellent in this style of skill development.

Training will be greatly hindered if the relationship is strained between teacher and student. The student needs to be in a relaxed, teachable state. Strained relationships distract from learning! Think about it. If someone is stressed because of a strained relationship, they're giving more mental energy to the problem of the tension of the strained relationship than learning skills. Daniel Goleman says it well: *"When emotionally upset, people cannot remember, attend, learn, or make decisions clearly. As one management consultant put it, Stress makes people stupid."*[4]

Training thrives in a "climate of self-assurance," a climate where trainees respect the integrity and capability of their leaders.

Teaching Style # 5. Mentoring

Mentoring is an ongoing relationship between a senior and junior employee. Mentoring provides guidance and a clear understanding of how the organization goes to achieve its vision and mission to the junior employee.

Mentors frequently double as executive coaches. They also serve as confidants, sounding boards, supportive listeners, guides, and tutors. A mentor may meet with the mentee less frequently than an executive coach. But mentoring sessions are normally longer and more far-ranging than coaching sessions.

Even the very best executives have mentors. Remember Alexander the Great? He slept with a copy of the Iliad under his pillow. He dreamt of becoming the new Achilles. In cases where the executive is new to the organization, a senior executive could be assigned as a mentor to assist the new executive settled into his role. Mentoring is one of the important methods for preparing them to be future executives. This method allows the mentor to determine what is required to improve the mentee's performance.

Once the mentor identifies the problem, weakness, and area that needs to be worked upon, the mentor can advise relevant training. The mentor can also provide opportunities to work on special processes and projects that master the skills.

Some key points in mentoring include attitude development. It is conducted for management-level employees. It focuses on identifying the weaknesses and the areas that need improvement, it is usually based on one-to-one interaction, and someone within the company does it.

Teaching Style # 6. Vestibule Training

Vestibule teaching is one of the on-the-process training where technical staff is educated on how to use equipment by developing a simulated workplace. This education is also termed 'close to the job schooling,' wherein a simulated work setup is created near the principal production plant. Professional and experienced teachers are assigned to educate workers on machinery and systems which are much like the real environment, a safe way to be used by them, rather than the real workplace. A flight simulator would be one good example. Another one would be a crane simulator device.

Vestibule schooling is performed in a schoolroom or computing device. This is either situated inside the central production unit or near to it. This type of training by assigning the learning personnel to expert trainers, reduces the burden of the supervisor tracking the entire training process. Vestibule education was more common in industries that use hands-on activities and specialized machines. It avoids fatal injuries and loss of life by ensuring the trainees are proficient before placing them in a live scenario in their workplace.

Benefits of Vestibule education

- It is the most effective training where many people are to be taught the essential skills.

- The actual work vicinity stays unaffected because vestibule education is accomplished at the simulated work setup rather than in the natural work vicinity.

- Trainees can focus with full attention, without fearing that their mistakes will affect production or other people's safety.

- Vestibule training is done by a dedicated trainer, rather than a supervisor on production. This usually ensures a dedicated training process.

- Trainees are at ease and learn without anxiety in preparation for the real workplace.

Disadvantages of Vestibule training

Vestibule schooling is often expensive, as the simulated workplace must be designed to imitate the actual workplace.

- It takes time to set up before the training can begin.

- Special trainers needed for vestibule training may be expensive as they are highly skilled individuals.

- Workers may also face difficulty settling in an actual work location.

Teaching Style # 7. Online Learning

Below are some benefits of online learning.

Flexible and Easy

Students have complex schedules; many students have challenging personal and professional lives. Because of this, traditional education is a challenge for these students as it requires them to relinquish their responsibilities and responsibilities to attend classes.

E-learning is different, as they can attend classes and learn whenever appropriate. They can also complete tasks whenever it suits them.

The flexibility provided by this teaching method allows students to further their education while attending to their responsibilities.

- Most online universities offer the same structure as their classrooms. You will take a class earlier in the week and be assigned a task. Then you will have a whole week to finish the given job. In addition, many institutions allow students to take courses at their own pace. You can fall behind for a few weeks if you have other obligations and take a break later. You can also go ahead and complete the whole course quickly.

- Several remote communities do not have the infrastructure to establish an educational institution. E-learning opens the door to further education for the people living in these areas. Anyone who wants to read can visit the library and use the internet to do an online study there. If they have an internet connection, they can learn from the comfort of their home.

- Many online learning courses offered by institutions charge the same monetary value as the physically present class. However, there are a few financial factors that make online learning cheaper. As you can learn anywhere and anytime, students do not need to quit their jobs. They also do not have to move or move around the center to learn.

- Students also save on meals abroad, which further reduces the financial burden of tuition at the institution.

- There are endless courses to choose from. If a student chooses to study online, he or she can be educated at an institution he or she would not otherwise have. In addition, students are not required to take their studies at the same institution. If another institution offers similar courses at a better price or an improved curriculum, you may choose to study there.

Below are some of the disadvantages of online learning.

Lack of Focus

- When away from the confines of a classroom, distraction is very easy. Many students do not have the discipline to study by themselves. The classroom environment provides a better environment to avoid distractions such as mobile phones, or other people who are not learning alongside the student. Students in a classroom environment can encourage each other, whereas a lone student left to themselves doesn't usually have that same benefit.

Reduced Student Support

- There is very little interaction between students in online classes. In addition, communication between students and teachers is declining. Because of this, students and teachers often feel isolated. This can lead to stress and anxiety, and students may feel they have no support. For schools to overcome this, administrators must encourage different types of communication between students and teachers. Video chats, emails, and online chats enable communication, reducing this feeling of isolation.

Preventing Cheating is Difficult

- Like regular classroom reading, online students need to be tested on what they have learned. But in general, no specialists or teachers are available to supervise students during exams. This often leads to students cheating on tests and sharing answers. This makes it difficult to assess students' knowledge accurately.

Additionally, if students know they can cheat to be successful, there is little reason to pay attention to the classroom and work hard to learn the lessons.

Too Much Screen time

- Spending too many hours looking at the screen can lead to eyestrain, headaches, and difficulty sleeping. In addition, spending many hours in front of a computer screen often leads to bad posture and all the health problems that come with bad posture.

Excessive use of screens is one of the essential factors in discouraging parents or employers from allowing their children or employees to study online. Giving students plenty of rest can help keep them physically and mentally clear.

Conclusion

Growing your collective skill set within your organization is essential. As we have seen, there are many ways to do this. Using the correct method of developing your combined skills would depend on many factors, including the student's learning style and the occupation within the business. Excellent knowledge of your product/service is one of the goals of leadership and gives you an advantage over your competitors.

NOTES

_____

_____

_____

_____

_____

_____

_____

_____

_____

_____

_____

_____

_____

_____

_____

_____

_____

_____

_____

_____

_____

_____

_____

_____

_____

_____

_____

_____

_____

_____

_____

_____

_____

_____

_____

_____

_____

_____

_____

_____

_____

_____

_____

_____

_____

_____

_____

CHAPTER FIVE

Essential Three-A Plan of How to Get There

INTRODUCTION

Planning how to get there is beneficial when starting out on a journey. This is the other essential regarding leadership. The leader has the vision but must communicate it to his team to be understood. There has to be continual progress toward that vision. One of the ways this is done is through staff meetings. Monitor progress through goals achieved in the past. Set goals and how they are to be completed in the short to medium-term future. Monitor performances and achievements from the past. Reward certain people and celebrate outstanding successes.

Discuss meetings in detail, such as how to get others involved and the option of missing a meeting. What are the consequences of people missing your meetings? Are they excused from your meetings if they have more pressing issues? Is it a good business practice to allow people to miss get-togethers? This will be answered in this chapter.

Staff meetings require planning. Can you meet too often? Who contributes to the planning? Once you've had the team meeting, what do you do afterward? How can you improve? These questions will all be answered.

STAFF MEETINGS THAT ENGAGE YOUR EMPLOYEES

Keep it Simple, Fun, and Focused.

Team meetings are an essential part of any successful group. But many organizations use group meetings ideas that fail to keep their personnel engaged, making them dull. People often attend out of a sense of duty instead of an exciting and effective encounter. Even with the online meeting options that so many people are taking advantage of these days, there are several ways to encourage engagement, camaraderie, and contribution.

Most team members, regardless of role, do not equate group meetings with either joy or a sense of achievement. Most people's impression of team meetings is "boring!" "Waste of my time!" "I could be working on my projects." Keep your personnel engaged if you are to inspire and preserve motivation and commitment in your staff.

If you can get some creativity in your meetings, it could be the catalyst that pushes attendees to get extra out of group meetings. Companies can draw on various techniques to boost their organizational meetings, using them as needed.

Inspirational team meetings can help group contributors get together and share ideas, propose, or check in on certain developments within the organization.

Without regular focus, a team can lose the organization's vision that they are working for. Conducting regular staff meetings helps keep your team focused on the idea and remain steadfast on long-term goals. Depending on the size of your staff team, implement a sensible timeframe that will enable adequate planning to prepare for the meeting.

Staff meetings require a careful blend of focusing on the vision and leading your people in that direction in small, achievable steps. Knowing your team is essential so you can customize the meetings as needed. When you become skilled at staff meetings, you will notice increased optimism, improved communication, and good suggestions being brought forward.

You do not often have all team members together who usually have the time or ability to meet. Make the most of this opportunity! This lets everyone know what is happening across different teams and departments. It will also align the organization's desires and obtain better information for their contributions toward them. Leaders can coach team members individually, but in a tailored way to teach the entire team about achieving the team's vision.

IMPORTANT GOALS TO KEEP IN MIND FOR STAFF MEETINGS

It is good to remind yourself and your team of these things whenever you get together for staff meetings.

- Review how well you and your team are tracking against your goals.

- Keep the team updated on developments on essential issues.

- Address any barriers that are being experienced.

- Discuss ideas that need addressing to come to solutions.

- And lastly, and most importantly, bring recognition to other team members who have performed well and honor them.

Staff meetings keep people informed and moving towards the same vision.

A well-planned meeting agenda increases team accountability and group engagement and enables creative problem-solving. People enjoy being both part of the problem-solving process and being productive.

Staff get-togethers are often opportunities to build camaraderie, so make this one of your aims.

When contemplating your staff meeting agenda, include these items:

- Team announcements and updates.

- Review past performances and objectives.

- Significant issues to address.

- Obstacles/Challenges.

- Present agenda.

EFFECTIVE STAFF MEETINGS

Determine Your Meeting Objective

The most important thing to remember is to determine the main objectives of your staff meeting. Determine to convey these points to your team so that you will be all like-minded regarding a common goal. If everyone agrees on the topics to be discussed, there will be a higher level of engagement.

While you can't please everyone, you should be able to reach a compromise to discuss the most pressing issues. The main agendas should be communicated through the meeting invite. The meeting should have a title and a description of the event so that everyone can clearly understand the objective of the meeting.

Discuss The Meeting Agenda in Advance

When inviting the team for the meeting, notify everyone that you will seek something from them for the schedule. This will give them time to think through the issues for them to contribute. Then, shortly before the meeting, call for their contributions to the plan from the team members.

Communicating the aim and pre-sending the program will help decide who will need to be at the meeting. If a person reads all the items and decides that they have no contribution to make, give them a choice to opt out of the meeting.

Make Meetings Optional

Making meetings optional appears to be terrible business practice. But here are some advantages:

- Making staff get-togethers voluntary eliminates excuses.

No one likes their time wasted in a needless staff meeting. No one can force you to attend a conference you deem a waste of time. All meetings are optional. However, experience sure does not give that impression!

By making it clear to everyone that all meetings are voluntary, you relieve people from making excuses. If there's work that is more important than the meeting, then do it. The company agreement perfectly understands that each person is accountable for using their time well. The leader of the meeting loses their excuse for holding mediocre meetings.

- Making meetings voluntary forces leaders to show their value.

When no one is forced to attend the meeting, and if anyone can leave, this will cause the meeting leader to show the value of the invitation. If they understand meetings are optional, it will force leaders to think if they could do without them, who could get the most out of it, and what the outcomes ought to be. Knowing this is essential for any first-rate staff get-togethers, but busy leaders regularly bypass this work if they know the staff will present themselves, regardless. Please eliminate the idea that your team will present themselves to an unproductive meeting and get rid of mediocre staff meetings.

- Making staff meetings voluntary help your core values.

By making meetings voluntary, organizations make it evident that the conference is not the point. This strategy tells employees that if it is a choice of team meetings or company values, company values need to win every time.

- Making meetings optional requires better note keeping.

For a meeting to be optional, it requires keeping good notes so that those who can't attend can catch up on what was missed. Although the person may have missed the meeting, they can still be informed through the notes.

- Making staff meetings optional makes them imperative to job performance.

A voluntary meeting policy does not suggest that conferences have no importance. Instead, discussions are one of the best tools for working towards your vision, growing alignment, solving troubles, and pushing momentum.

Instead, this policy makes each person accountable for making the best use of meeting time. If leaders fail to run valuable meetings and the staff does not go, this will significantly impact performance. Suppose a team member decides not to go to the conference, thereby failing to make contributions, thoughts, solutions, and facts to the organization. In that case, their value to the agency decreases dramatically.

There are two primary sources of performance failure in teams without this policy. Leaders frequently fail to make the best use of everyone's time, and employees fail to make contributions.

Concentrate on what you wish to discuss for the meeting. To do that right, have some informal discussions with relevant colleagues to decide what they think is essential. Share your plan with a timeline that allocates various minutes to each item. Give this to people in advance so they can arrive prepared. Once you're in the meeting, stick with the scheduled items and time given. This prevents contributors from wandering off subject matter and enables the group to complete the meeting on time.

Encourage all to contribute

Good leaders are aware of the bias that people can have. Everyone has different life experiences, perspectives, and thoughts to contribute to the team. It is wisdom to get all involved.

Embrace the idea that everyone should be valued (and there are no wrong opinions). Inspire your crew to talk up where all feel welcome to contribute. Encourage the typically quieter attendees to contribute by writing down their ideas before the meeting and encouraging their thoughts. When you inspire the team to speak up, you create an environment where all feel welcome to contribute. You may be surprised how much confidence and encouragement this could give someone.

Delegate The Next Steps

Think about what needs to be undertaken next week. Prioritize your commitments that need to be completed. Assign them to specific people who carry out these duties. When you assign responsibilities in a meeting, it will help to hold each other accountable. It could also help you support each other by building teamwork.

One of your colleagues may be overwhelmed with too much to do. But someone may have some room to take on someone else's load if they're overloaded. When you delegate actionable items, it will keep you organized and on top of your day-to-day responsibilities. Keep note of who is doing the delegated tasks and what date they will be done. Communication and accountability are the foundation for high-achieving teams.

Ask for Feedback from Your Team to Improve Your Meetings

If you want to back your team to succeed, you need to create a lifestyle where giving, receiving, and enforcing feedback is a part of the DNA. Nobody has arrived at the fount of all knowledge. We should all be eager to learn through feedback from our colleagues.

Receiving feedback from your meetings can help you know if your team is finding your sessions valuable and if there are some things you can do to improve.

You can ask a few questions:

- Are the meetings too often or too infrequent?

- Should they be shorter or longer?

- Did we make the best use of our time?

- Did we miss anything?

Working together with your team gives you the prospect of gaining their insights and feedback. This will help you discover better approaches to staff meetings and maximize your efficiency in getting your team to where you are seeking to lead them in your vision.

Frequency of Meetings

Decisions need to be made on the frequency of the meetings. There is a term that is used in this context: Cadence. It refers to the meeting rhythm. Imagine a set of rowers on a boat. You are setting a pace to get the maximum amount of work done per stroke. A meeting rhythm, or cadence, should be timed to get the total amount of work done between meetings. Place the panels too far apart, and people will begin to drift and lose focus. Place the meetings too close together, and you lose valuable time that could have been working towards your vision.

Senior management usually meets more often, usually weekly. Followed by supervisors/intermediate leaders, and finally, all people usually every quarter.

CONCLUSION

We've seen how important staff meetings are in navigating toward your vision or reviewing the organization's past performance.

We have seen some ways to engage your members to prevent boredom.

We have seen the benefits of making meetings optional. We have observed putting the onus on the meeting organizer to ensure that they are needed and not a waste of people's time. It was also refreshing to see someone could put the company's values first, miss a meeting, if needed, and use the notes from the record-keeping raised to a higher standard because of making meetings optional.

NOTES

_____

_____

_____

_____

_____

_____

_____

_____

_____

_____

_____

_____

_____

_____

_____

_____

_____

CHAPTER SIX

Essential Four-The Mentoring Program-the Art of Building Relationships

INTRODUCTION

Mentoring is the relational aspect of the connection between the leader, team, and team members. In my definition, I claim that "leadership is the art of building relationships towards a goal." Mentoring happens within the atmosphere of good leadership. Some famous people knew this aspect thousands of years ago, but it has only recently been rediscovered.

How well you lead will be determined by how well you know your product/service and the quality of your relationships within the team you lead. I will show you that the best leaders successfully combine both aspects, knowing your product/service and building strong relationships between them and their team members. Also, great leaders keep relationships healthy amongst all team members, bringing peace and harmony to team members. They stop bullying and unite the team to a common cause.

A perfect example was Alexander the Great. I believe that he is one of the very few leaders who operated powerfully in all four leadership essentials. The Greeks and Macedonians were rivals for centuries, and he crushed a revolt from the Greeks. But he sought to use this as an opportunity to bring unity and a shared vision. He appealed to them with this quote:

"Holy shadows of the dead, I'm not to blame for your cruel and bitter fate, but the accursed rivalry which brought sister nations and brother people to fight one another. I do not feel happy for this victory of mine. On the contrary, I would be glad, brothers, if I had all of you standing here next to me, since we are united by the same language, the same blood, and the same visions." [1]

CREATE AN ENVIRONMENT WHERE EVERYONE CAN SHINE

Learning from some of history's best leaders, Sun Tzu and Alexander the Great, we can see the value of building great relationships.

Let's think again about Alexander the Great: Without a doubt, Alexander's extraordinary people skills enabled him to do great exploits. The great Aristotle mentored him. Today, most people would classify Aristotle as a philosophy teacher, not realizing that he taught people skills. Most people don't understand the added talent that this gave him. We regard philosophy as something enjoyable, optional, but not essential. What have values and relationship skills got to do with war? What person would think of adding relationship skills to your education to become a history-making General?

Most people would think, "You're a General. Give the orders, and then if they don't follow through, let them receive their due punishments!" But considering my definition of leadership, "the art of building relationships towards a goal," the teaching of values would be an outstanding asset. It's worthwhile to look at some of Aristotle's quotes to observe the emotional intelligence he passed on to Alexander.

- *"Anybody can become angry - that is easy, but to be angry with the right person and to the right degree and at the right time and for the right purpose, and in the right way - that is not within everybody's power and is not easy."*[2]

- *"Educating the mind without educating the heart is no education at all."*[3] (From this quote, you could be accurately proved that Aristotle was the father of Emotional Intelligence.)

- *"The most important relationship we can all have is the one you have with yourself, the most important journey you can take is one of self-discovery. To know yourself, you must spend time with yourself; you must not be afraid to be alone. Knowing yourself is the beginning of all wisdom."*[4]

- *"Today, see if you can stretch your heart and expand your love so that it touches not only those to whom you can give it easily but also to those who need it so much."*[5]

- *"The high-minded man does not bear grudges, for it is not the mark of a great soul to remember injuries but to forget them."*[6]

Because of this great teaching from Aristotle, Alexander had excellent people skills to build a team through which he could transition his vision into reality.

CONTENTED WORKERS ARE MORE PRODUCTIVE

A detailed study of happiness and productivity has discovered that contented workers are thirteen percent more productive. The research was performed within the operation center of British telecoms firm BT for six months through Jan-Emmanuel De Neve (Saïd business college, college of Oxford), George Ward (MIT), and Clement Bellet (Erasmus college Rotterdam).

It was discovered that when workers are happier, they work faster by making more calls per hour and converting more calls to sales.

The authors state that, while the link between happiness and productivity has often been a theory, this study gives the first convincing evidence for this relationship. There has never been such definite proof as this study that you are more productive when content.

Recent research into the attitude of the United Kingdom has determined that paid work is ranked close to the lowest in an activity that makes society happy. There seems to be large room for improvement in employees' happiness while they are at work. Although this benefits the workers themselves, the study showed it's also within the interests of their employers.

"The BT workers were asked to rate their happiness on a weekly basis for six months using a simple email survey containing five emoji buttons representing states of happiness–from very sad to very happy. Data on attendance, call-to-sale conversion, and customer satisfaction were tracked, along with the worker's scheduled hours and breaks. The researchers collated this information alongside administrative data obtained from the firm on worker characteristics, work schedules and productivity."[7] The researchers found that happy workers do not work more hours than their discontented colleagues–they are simply more productive within their time at work.

A LEADER NEEDS TO BELIEVE IN HIS PEOPLE

Confidence in the ones you lead is the hallmark of a great leader. Best-selling leadership expert John C. Maxwell agrees with this character quality, *"a key to empowering others is high belief in people."*8. Coaching, inspiring, guiding, correcting, and celebrating individuals to become their best is a duty of all leaders. It is one of the most satisfying aspects of being a leader. Continue to believe in your team, even though you may see their slip-ups. We all have our share of mistakes along the way. The heart of a leader makes a genuine effort to have faith in the people he/she leads.

Here are some historical examples of great mentors whose leaders made them into greatness:

Cus D'Amato

Cus D'Amato was made famous by training Mike Tyson. He also mentored Floyd Patterson and José Torres, all of whom went to be inducted into the International Boxing Hall of Fame. He also trained several successful boxing trainers, including Teddy Atlas and Kevin Rooney.

Cus D'Amato And Mike Tyson

Cus D'Amato met Mike when he was around 12/13 as a troubled youth in a boys' reform school. After Tyson's mother died, Cus adopted Mike. (Do you see building a relationship here?) Tyson credits D'Amato with building his confidence and guiding him as a father figure.

He convinced Mike Tyson that he could be a world-class boxer. Cus said to him, *"you could be champion of the world."* [9]

And Cus didn't just say that to him once or twice. He kept telling him, even though Mike didn't believe it was possible. In Mike Tyson's own words, *"this guy's really crazy... he's crazy"* [10]

Eventually, Cus's belief in Mike broke through. Cus D'Amato said, *"A boy comes to me with a spark of interest. I feed the spark and it becomes a flame.*

I feed the flame and it becomes a fire. I feed the fire and it becomes a roaring blaze." [11]

Who is the more excellent person here? Cus D'Amato or Mike Tyson, one of the greatest heavyweight boxing champions of the world? Without a doubt, it was Cus. Without him, Mike Tyson would not have recognized the talent inside him. To quote Cus D'Amato again; *"Greatness is not a measure of how great you are but how great others came to be because of you"* [12]

Many years later, as Joe Rogan was suggesting to Mike Tyson the possibility of training a younger vision of himself, Mike replied, *"it takes more to be a great trainer than a great fighter."* [13]

Many leaders have the mentality of a gang member that "greatness is their turf, and they better not reach past me or my potential!" But the truth is, it takes a great deal of effort to mentor someone into greatness, and the rewards are fantastic! It is not for selfish or insecure leaders. If you have the mentality of training someone to go further than you, you will be in great demand. You must have a generous heart for this. It is against our selfish human nature to have a desire for someone to succeed beyond our achievements. But that is where the real growth is for you as a leader. The quote from Cus D'Amato earlier echoes what another great leader, the late President Ronald Reagan, said, *"The greatest leader is not necessarily the one who does the greatest things. He is the one that gets the people to do the greatest things."* [14]

Alexander the Great

He wasn't deterred even though he was vastly outnumbered by the world super-power of the time. He convinced his people that they were more than capable of doing extraordinary feats. If his men didn't come through, that would mean death for him and his soldiers! He said to his people, *"On their side, more men are standing, on ours, more will fight!"* [15]

It takes a secure leader, with a generous heart to bring out a champion in someone, to become so successful that he outshines the leader himself. These people are rare and are the real champions. Having another person believe in you gives you confidence. Best-selling author on leadership, Simon Sinek has confirmed this highly valued quality of believing in those you lead with this quote:

"Leadership is about empowering others to achieve things they did not think possible." [16]

EMOTIONAL INTELLIGENCE

Mentoring people requires people skills, of which some leaders are bankrupt in this regard. They are way too confident in their knowledge of their product/service only. Their team follows them because they have no choice. They need their income. If people don't get it they will not eat or have a roof over their heads. But people skills are an art that can be learned. IQ (Intelligence Quotient) and EQ (Emotional Quotient) determine how well you do in your life and career. IQ alone is not enough; EQ also matters.

Psychologists generally agree that IQ accounts for roughly 20% of the ingredients required for success. The rest depends on everything else—including EQ. Think of it this way: your I.Q is used to build your knowledge around your product/service, and you use your E.Q to develop your relationships in your team as you all head towards your goal.

Successful people have a high level of Emotional Intelligence. They have refined the art of building relationships as they lead people towards the vision/goal. Greatness is often where E.Q and I.Q are combined. One definition of Emotional Intelligence is: *"being able to recognize, understand and manage our own emotions and recognize, understand, and influence the emotions of others.*

In practical terms, this means being aware that emotions can drive our behavior and impact people (positively and negatively) and learning how to manage those emotions – both our own and others.

Managing emotions is especially important in situations when we are under pressure. For example, when we are...

- *Giving and receiving feedback*

- *Meeting tight deadlines*

- *Dealing with challenging relationships*

- *Not having enough resources*

- *Navigating change*

- *Working through setbacks and failure."* [17]

The importance of Emotional Intelligence has been recognized in high-level business management. *"Some studies show that companies that invest in boosting employees' EI have returns on that investment up to four times what they put in."* [18]

THE FOUR DOMAINS OF EMOTIONAL INTELLIGENCE

The Harvard Business Review chose his article "What Makes a Leader" as one of the 10 'must-read' articles from its pages. Republished in his new collection of works, Goleman takes us through the fundamentals of leadership.

Daniel Goleman – "What Makes a Leader"

"Well, there are four domains of emotional intelligence, and that article marches us through each one," he says.

- *"The first is self-awareness, and self-awareness is an impressive set of abilities because first of all it's invisible to people, it's subtle, and it's also highly underrated. Self-awareness is essential for the other three domains.*

- *The second is self-management, if you don't know what's going on inside yourself, you will be very poor at managing others. It's about having the ability to control your own emotions, so they don't block your ability to think well, to create, to innovate, to stay fixed on a goal, and the drive to achieve. Those are self-management skills.*

- *Empathy is the third, and it again requires good self-awareness. There's a lot of research even at the level of brain function that shows that people who are low in self-awareness are not able to attune to other people, not able to read them.*

- *And the fourth domain in emotional intelligence is social skills. This last is about managing relationships, and it involves the most apparent leadership skills–things like persuasion, influence, communication, elaboration, and teamwork.*

So, what you're doing is putting together your ability to manage yourself, your ability to read the other person and know what to do and what to say next, to be skillful interpersonally–and those three all build from self-awareness.

My associates in the Hay Group have some authentic data now showing that leaders who are low in self-awareness typically fail to be able to develop strengths in these other domains," he says. [20]

When thinking about the first domain of emotional intelligence mentioned here, I'm reminded of a quote from Aristotle, *"The most important relationship we can all have is the one you have with yourself, the most important journey you can take is one of self-discovery. To know yourself, you must spend time with yourself; you must not be afraid to be alone. Knowing yourself is the beginning of all wisdom."* [21]

A Historical Example of High and Low E.Q.

A leadership example of emotional intelligence at the extremes is in the Bible. (For those who are not God-fearing, relax. This is simply a historical example. This is a secular book.) One is highly intelligent, and the other is seriously lacking. Eli and Elisha. Two different leaders and the contrasts of their E.Q. could not be more extreme. Before we go there, let's look at Proverbs 18:2 (ISV); *"Fools find no pleasure in understanding but delight in airing their own opinions."* One aspect of emotional intelligence is understanding other people's emotions about their situations. [22]

Eli in 1 Samuel 1:10 (ISV); *"Deeply distressed, she prayed to the Lord and wept bitterly. Hannah made a vow: 'Lord of the Heavenly Armies, if you just look at the misery of your maidservant, remember me, and don't forget your maidservant. If you give your maidservant a son, then I'll give him to the Lord for all the days of his life, and a razor is never to touch his head.'*

As she continued to pray in the Lord's presence, Eli was watching her mouth. Hannah was praying inwardly. Her lips were quivering, and her voice could not be heard. So, Eli thought she was drunk. Eli told her, 'How long will you stay drunk? Put away your wine!'

'No, sir!' Hannah replied. "I'm a deeply troubled woman. I've drunk neither wine nor beer. I've been pouring out my soul in the Lord's presence. Don't

consider your maidservant a worthless woman. Rather, all this time I've been speaking because I'm very anxious and distressed.'

'Go in peace,' Eli answered. 'May the God of Israel grant the request you have asked of him.'" (1 Samuel 1:10-17, ISV.) [23]

And now let's look at an extreme on the other end of reading people's emotions. The context of this story is a woman's son dies, and she rushes to tell Elisha, the prophet of Israel at the time, but she doesn't tell him the details. As she came near the man of God on the mountain, she grabbed his feet. When Gehazi intervened to push her away, the man of God said, *"Leave her alone! She is deeply troubled! The Lord has concealed the thing from me and hasn't informed me."* (2 Kings 4:27. ISV) He can see that she's going through intense emotional pain through her body language. Like Eli, his assistant Gehazi is completely ignorant of her pain. Now, which leader would you like to serve with?[24]

THE ART OF CRITIQUING YOUR TEAM

Nobody likes to bring correction. Some people are exceptions. Those who love to bring correction are people who thrive on power over people. However, there are serious consequences of not bringing correction. I've heard that those who enjoy bringing correction should not be the ones to bring it. There is an art in bringing correction without discouragement. I've heard that bringing correction the right way is like "stepping on someone's shoes without taking the shine from them." I find that it is easier to bring correction if I do it in love. I endeavor to have the highest regard for the person. I speak the truth in love. If we bring correction (truth) in love, the majority of the time it is well received. Consider this from an experienced business advisor:

Harry Levinson, a psychoanalyst turned corporate consultant, gives the following advice on the art of critique, which is intricately entwined with the art of praise:

- *"Be specific. Pick a significant incident, an event that illustrates a key problem that needs changing, or a pattern of deficiency, such as the inability to do certain parts of a job well. It demoralizes people just to hear that they are doing something wrong without knowing what the specifics are so they can change.*

- *"Specificity," Levinson points out, "is just as important for praise as for criticism. I won't say that vague praise has no effect at all, but it doesn't have much, and you can't learn from it."*

- *Offer a solution. The critique, like all useful feedback, should point to a way to fix the problem. Otherwise, it leaves the recipient frustrated, demoralized, or demotivated.*

- *Be present. Critiques, like praise, are effective face to face and in private. People who are uncomfortable giving criticism—or offering praise—are likely to ease the burden on themselves by doing it at a distance, such as in a memo. But this makes the communication too impersonal and robs the person receiving it of an opportunity for a response or clarification.*

- *Be sensitive. This is a call for empathy, for being attuned to the impact of what you say and how you say it on the person at the receiving end. Managers who have little empathy," Levinson points out, "are most prone to giving feedback in a hurtful fashion, such as the withering put-down. The net effect of such criticism is destructive: instead of opening the way for a corrective, it creates an emotional backlash of resentment, bitterness, defensiveness, and distance."* 25.

Correction should preferably be done in private. Many managers get off on correcting people publicly and feel empowered at the other person's expense. Of course, there are times when you need to correct people publicly. But it is better to correct people privately if possible. I once witnessed a brilliant supervisor get this perfect. He noticed an incident that needed addressing. (The bullying of another staff member.) He spoke to the individual personally on a one-to-one basis. He warned him that he would not tolerate this sort of behavior. At the next team meeting, he described the situation to everyone, but kept his name anonymous. So, he protected the individual's honor and dignity but notified the team that bullying of another staff member would not be tolerated.

BULLYING FROM THE LEADERSHIP

I have seen some very destructive leadership styles in my visits to various workplaces. With one company, staff morale was extremely low on two different sites that I visited. Occasionally, I witnessed subordinates being disciplined harshly over minor mistakes. For example, they had a policy of correcting staff over minor incidents by sending them home for several days off. They were employed on a temporary basis. Without any written warnings! I felt sorry for them. I hope they weren't living from paycheck to paycheck and had little children to feed. This style of extreme discipline happened with this same company on two different sites. If this is not bullying, then what is?

On one occasion, one of the supervisors proclaimed at a team meeting, "If you're not happy working here, you can f#%* off! This company had a high staff turnover, and both projects went overdue for more than a year. They had a false economy of hiring temporary staff, thinking they would save money by not paying them when they did not need them. But people need a place of belonging and job security.

Remember, that contented staff is more productive! Also, there was a lawsuit from a subcontractor, and they had financial penalties for going over the allocated time. Sometimes people can have unfortunate circumstances. There can be unforeseen problems with specific projects. But a consistently high turnover of staff and a lack of productivity, and lawsuits from disgruntled subcontractors is a management problem.

A famous quote says, *"employees don't leave companies; they leave bad managers."* According to most research, employees who rate supervisor performance as average are four times more likely to look for a new job. Harsh or antagonistic leadership can be a significant source of stress for the team members. On the other hand, supportive and skilled managers can encourage loyalty and high performance. Leaders play a massive role in shaping the employee experience and ensuring it is as pleasant and productive as possible.

The way you fix this is by providing managers with mentoring and ongoing training to expand their relationship skills. You conduct regular team reviews with anonymous surveys and hold leaders responsible for the people in their immediate care.

Managers can improve their relationship skills by reading books on leadership. They can also serve as leaders in volunteer organizations on weekends if they have time. For example, by coaching one of their favorite sports. The style of leadership when volunteering must be done through the power of persuasion, not through force. People can leave voluntary organizations easily because it is not critical for survival. However, earning a living is different because people have bills to pay and need their income. So, exerting force in paid employment may be easy, but it's not a good test of your leadership. Sun Tzu's quote, *"A leader leads by example, not by force,"* [26] is so accurate!

Examples of Bullying from the Leadership

- Addressing someone with foul language or any form of verbal abuse.

- Degrading or demeaning comments that might include insults or name-calling.

- Harsh criticism in the presence of other employees.

- Unnecessarily raising one's voice, e.g., shouting at a subordinate.

- Conduct that diminishes psychological protection, including withholding essential job-related information, refusing to answer questions, or refusing to help while requested.

- Consistently making unfavorable or unreasonable tasks.

- Retaliation against a whistleblower.

- Using position or authority to speak down to or demean any subordinates.

- Deliberate exclusion of people from meetings or events they should be attending.

- Ostracism, exclusion, or the use of silent treatment.

- Setting someone up to fail.

- Withholding important project-related information.

- Excessive discipline for minor mistakes.

- Racial, ethnic, sexual, gender, or spiritual slurs.

- Circulating personal correspondence (emails, messages, texts) without permission.

- Rude nonverbal behaviors or gestures (e.g., eye-rolling, snickering, finger-pointing, staring).

- Taking credit for the work of someone else.

- Gossiping or rumor spreading.

There is absolutely no room for any of this terrible behavior. It stifles creativity and destroys productivity. Leaders should be setting an example. A toxic work environment is where people are more prone to make mistakes or lose productivity. Daniel Goleman says, *"When emotionally upset, people cannot remember, attend, learn, or make decisions clearly. As one management consultant put it, 'Stress makes people stupid.'"* [27]

From this quote, you could effectively argue that excess stress could potentially increase workplace accidents through workplace stress, "making them stupid." Interestingly, I recall asking a tow truck driver about his busiest day. He said, "always Friday night. People are at their most stressed point of the week, and their minds are not on driving. They're more prone to make mistakes."

A COMPARISON OF TYRANTS VERSUS LEADERS

Tyrants

- Tyrants lead through fear.

- Tyrants embarrass, humiliate, or harshly correct their team members frequently and openly in front of others.

- Tyrants make subordinates feel stupid.

- Tyrants let you know that they can easily replace you.

- Tyrants continually remind people that they are superior (through their position or achievements.)

- Tyrants are incredibly self-centered.

- Tyrants are extremely low on Emotional Intelligence.

- Tyrants repeatedly say, "You're lucky to have a job."

- Tyrants give orders.

- Tyrants create an underlying current of fear and suspicion.

Leaders

- Leaders lead through inspiration/influence.

- Leaders correct in private, discretely, or diplomatically.

- Leaders give their subordinates confidence.

- Leaders let you know you're needed or valuable.

- Leaders talk about their achievements sparingly. They're secure, they don't need to show off.

- Leaders are generous, kind, and other-centered.

- Leaders are highly Emotionally Intelligent.

- Leaders politely request.

- Leaders create a team with unity and trust amongst each other.

Conclusion of The Mentoring Program

We have seen the need for developing an environment in a group of people where they can shine. We observed this through the outstanding people skills in great leaders like Sun Tzu and Alexander the Great. It was Aristotle who mentored Alexander and instilled such a high degree of Emotional Intelligence.

We established what sort of environment for people to be at their best. We saw convincing evidence in a study that found contented workers are 13% more productive. It was not that they worked longer hours, but that they were more productive with their work time. Contented workers are in the best interests of employers.

Next, we looked at the relationship skill of believing in people. Coaching, inspiring, guiding, correcting, and celebrating individuals to become their most significant potential is what a great leader does. A leader makes a genuine effort to see the best in the ones they are mentoring. We saw this first in Cus D' Amato, who instilled confidence in Mike Tyson to become a world heavyweight boxing champion. You could say that believing in people increases their confidence and sense of contribution to the company, creating contented workers. This is a win for employers and employees.

We saw Alexander the Great's belief in his army. The Persians greatly outnumbered him, but without any doubt, he had great confidence in his army. If they didn't come through for him, it would have meant death!

After this, we looked at Emotional Intelligence and remembered that psychologists generally agree that IQ accounts for roughly 20% of the ingredients required for success. We observed that emotions could drive our behavior and impact people (positively and negatively) and the importance of managing those emotions–both our own and others.

We saw that companies that invest in boosting employees' Emotional Intelligence have returns on that investment up to four times what they put in.

Following this, we observed bullying from the leadership. We are reminded that people's productivity suffers in an area of bullying, as I witnessed productivity targets not being met. On both sites where bullying was evident, projects went more than a year overdue. Finally, we made a comparison of leaders versus tyrants. It was obvious which one had put the work into developing the people skills necessary to get a team working together in harmony.

Summary of Leadership Condensed into Four Essentials

Many leaders are great at knowing their product/service. They know it better than most people in their industry. Unfortunately, this is only one of the four essentials of leadership, and far too many rely on this one pillar. I believe that I have shown convincing proof of my claim that "leadership is the art of building relationships towards a goal." After these two, the third is the knowledge of your product/service, and the fourth is a plan for getting there. Rarely will you find a leader operating powerfully in all four leadership essentials!

Alexander The Great and Sun Tzu were both great leaders who changed the world through their achievements and the people they motivated. Their leadership is still studied throughout the world today. I believe that I have shown that both outstanding leaders operated using all four leadership essentials. Knowing this, leaders can no longer use their positions of power to intimidate their teams. They are relying only on intimidation for leadership influence.

It's time for all managers, leaders, coaches, etc., to look at the people under their supervision and their relationships. Are you relying exclusively on the knowledge of your product/service only? Have you left the relational aspect out of leading a team? Do you use threats to manipulate people? Does your organization keep records of staff turnover? If people are leaving because of bad management, how will you know? Remember! Contented teams are more productive.

As you'll recall, we looked at Alexander the Great and learned that leadership leads from the front by example. Sun Tzu also shared these relationship skills, who stated, "a leader leads by example, and not by force."

We looked in detail at the essential leadership element of having a vision and being able to articulate it into a vision statement.

We saw how this is like a map to keep us on course. We looked at the distinction between a Vision and Mission Statement. We discovered that vision looks into the future, but a mission statement looks at the present and what we are doing here and now.

After studying the essential of having a Vision, we made clear the necessity of growing your skills within your organization. We looked at various ways to develop your skills, including recruiting, on-the-job training, job rotation, apprenticeship, coaching, mentoring, vestibule learning, and e-learning. We discussed the pros and cons of each. Good leaders pass on their knowledge of their product/service because they know it gives them an edge over the competition. We observed that a good leader knows what their team is capable of. We noted that growing your collective skill set within your organization is vital to staying ahead of your rivals.

The next pillar of leadership we reviewed was a plan to get there. We studied staff meetings and discovered they are essential in keeping on track in working towards your vision. We noted creative ways to prevent boredom, such as celebrating people's achievements and honoring them before others as they progress towards the vision.

Another discovery was that it is permissible for people not to attend staff meetings. We saw that it increased the quality of the record-keeping and lifted the standard of company get-togethers. We observed cadence, the balance between too many staff meetings and not enough, that there is a sweet spot that brings the best compromise between productivity and planning. We learned the art of bringing people together to discuss the plan and keep the discussions on track.

Within my definition of leadership, I claimed that *"leadership is the art of building relationships towards a goal."* Mentoring is essential in good leadership. It is the relational aspect of it. We have seen Cus D'Amato's impact on Mike Tyson, of how his belief in him enabled him to see something that Mike couldn't see in himself. Alexander and Sun Tzu also built great relationships with their men, leading them from the front of the battle lines and by example.

Also, great leaders keep relationships healthy amongst the team members. They have tremendous confidence in their team, inspiring them to achieve great works. We noted that a great leader is not threatened by someone going further than them. They also bring peace and harmony to the team members. They stop bullying and unite the team to a common cause.

One of my aims in writing this book is to make it easy enough to understand for those just starting in leadership and yet have a lot of treasure for those who are seasoned leaders.

The ultimate goal of a leader is to train someone up to replace you. This takes security. But ultimately, this will make you an in-demand, high-value person. If you have this attitude, you're irreplaceable! Remembering the words of Cus D'Amato, *"Greatness is not a measure of how great you are but how great others came to be because of you."*[28]

Study your product/service. I hope I've motivated you to mentor someone in your workplace. Build relationships. The world has plenty of people who give orders, but few mature people are willing to walk with those who long to develop their skills. If this book has helped you, please tell others about it!

NOTES

_____

_____

_____

_____

_____

_____

_____

_____

_____

_____

_____

_____

_____

_____

_____

_____

_____

_____

_____

_____

_____

_____

_____

_____

_____

_____

_____

_____

_____

_____

_____

Notes

_____

_____

_____

_____

_____

_____

_____

_____

_____

_____

_____

_____

_____

_____

_____

_____

_____

_____

_____

_____

_____

_____

_____

_____

_____

_____

_____

_____

_____

_____

_____

_____

_____

_____

_____

_____

_____

_____

_____

_____

_____

_____

_____

_____

_____

_____

_____

_____

_____

_____

_____

_____

_____

_____

_____

_____

_____

_____

_____

_____

_____

_____

Endnotes

Chapter 1

1. Simon Sinek. Article title: "500 QUOTES BY SIMON SINEK [PAGE - 3]: A-Z Quotes

https://www.azquotes.com/author/13643-Simon_Sinek?p=3

Website title A Date accessed December 17, 2021.

2. Article title: 101 Colin Powell Quotes on Leadership & Success

https://succeedfeed.com/colin-powell-quotes/

Website title: Succeed Feed

Date accessed: February 26, 2022

Date published: November 30, 2018.

3. Goleman, Daniel. Emotional Intelligence.

Book title: Emotional intelligence

Book publisher: Bantam Books

Publication year 2020 Page 133.

4. Article title: A quote by Bill Gates

https://www.goodreads.com/quotes/12422-as-we-look-ahead-into-the-next-century-leaders-will

Website titleGoodreads

Date accessedMay 13, 2022.

5. Article title: What is Leadership? The ultimate guide: Tony Robbins

https://www.tonyrobbins.com/what-is-leadership/

Website titletonyrobbins.com

Date accessedMay 13, 2022.

6. Article title: Leadership is the capacity to translate vision into reality - In Focus - Manara Global

https://www.manaraglobal.com/in-focus-news/2019/5/7/leadership-is-the-capacity-to-translate-vision-into-reality

Website title: Manara Global. Reputation Management, Communications & PR.

Date accessed May 13, 2022

Date published May 08, 2022.

7. Book title: The Inspirational Leader: inspire your team to believe in the impossible

Book publisher Leadership First Publication year 2019 Page 20.

Chapter 2. Examples of Great Leaders

1. Article title: A quote from The Art of War

https://www.goodreads.com/quotes/492309-treat-your-men-as-you-would-your-own-beloved-sons Website title Goodreads. Date accessed: February 28, 2022

2. Article title: A quote by Sun Tzu

https://www.goodreads.com/quotes/157821-when-one-treats-people-with-benevolence-justice-and-righteoousness-and Website titleGoodreads. Date accessed: February 28, 2022.

3. Article title: A quote from The Art of War

https://www.goodreads.com/quotes/418148-if-soldiers-are-punished-before-they-have-grown-attached-to

Website title Goodreads. Date accessed: February 28, 2022.

4. Article title: A quote from The Art of War

https://www.goodreads.com/quotes/17976-if-you-know-the-enemy-and-know-yourself-you-need

Website title Goodreads Date accessed: February 28, 2022.

5. Article title: A quote from The Art of War

https://www.goodreads.com/quotes/17973-victorious-warriors-win-first-and-then-go-to-war-while

Website title Goodreads. Date accessed: February 28, 2022.

6. Article title: The Art of War Quotes by Sun Tzu

https://www.goodreads.com/work/quotes/3200649

Website title Goodreads. Date accessed: February 28, 2022.

7. Article title: A quote from The Art of War

https://www.goodreads.com/quotes/3213455-a-leader-leads-by-example-not-by-force

Website title: Goodreads. Date accessed: March 7, 2022.

8. Article title: Erwin Rommel Quote

https://libquotes.com/erwin-rommel/quote/lbw4j4u

Website title: Lib Quotes. Date accessed: December 13, 2021.

9. Article title: A quote from The Art of War

https://www.goodreads.com/quotes/7048129-regard-your-soldiers-as-your-children-and-they-will-follow

Website title: Goodreads. Date accessed: March 02, 2022.

10. Article title: Infantry Attacks Quotes by Erwin Rommel

https://www.goodreads.com/work/quotes/243059-infanterie-greift-an

Website title: Goodreads. Date accessed: February 28, 2022.

11. Article title: Quote by Alexander the Great

https://www.quoteslyfe.com/quote/There-are-no-more-worlds-to-conquer-218560

Website title: Quoteslyfe. Date accessed: February 25, 2022.

12. Article title: The 6 Leadership Secrets of Alexander the Great

http://ancientheroes.net/blog/leadership-secrets-alexander

Website title: Ancient Heroes. Date accessed: December 13, 2021

Date published: April 27, 2016.

13. Article title: A quote by Alexander the Great

https://www.goodreads.com/quotes/903137-youths-of-the-pellaians-and-of-the-macedonians-and-of

Website title: Goodreads. Date accessed: February 25, 2022.

14. Article title: A quote by C.S. Lewis

https://www.goodreads.com/quotes/8188266-hardships-often-prepare-ordinary-people-for-an-extraordinary-destiny

Website title: Goodreads. Date accessed: July 11, 2022.

15. Article title: "We of Macedon for generations…" Alexander the Great Quote

https://www.quotescosmos.com/quotes/Alexander-the-Great-quote-3.html

Website title: Quotes Cosmos. Date accessed: December 13, 2021. Date published: July 31, 2021.

16. Article title: Alexander the Great Quote

https://www.azquotes.com/quote/551168

Website title: A. Date accessed: December 13, 2021.

17. Article title: Alexander the Great Quotes: Keep Inspiring Me

https://www.keepinspiring.me/alexander-the-great-quotes/

Website title: KeepInspiring.me. Date accessed: December 13, 2021

Date published: June 26, 2021.

18. Article title: Alexander the Great Quotes to Inspire You to Do the Impossible

https://everydaypower.com/alexander-the-great-quotes/

Website title: Everyday Power. Date accessed: December 13, 2021.

Date published: June 16, 2021.

19. Article title: Alexander the Great Quote

https://libquotes.com/alexander-the-great/quote/lbg2u9r

Website title: Lib Quotes. Date accessed: December 13, 2021.

Article title: 50 Inspiring Alexander the Great Quotes On Fear

URL: https://quotestospark.com/alexander-the-great-quotes-on-fear/

Website title: Quotes to Spark. Date accessed: December 13, 2021.

Date published: November 23, 2020.

Chapter 3. Essential # 1) A Goal / Vision

1. Article title: 30 Steve Jobs Leadership Quotes to Help You Achieve Success in Life

https://marketmegood.com/blog/steve-jobs-leadership-quotes/

Website title: 30 Steve Jobs Leadership Quotes to Help You Achieve Success in Life

Date accessed: May 20, 2022. Date published: January 02, 2021.

2. Article title: Purpose & Company Vision

https://www.coca-colacompany.com/company/purpose-and-vision

Website title: The Coca-Cola Company. Date accessed: January 07, 2022.

3. Article title: General Motors Mission Statement 2022: General Motors Mission & Vision Analysis

https://mission-statement.com/general-motors/

Website titleGeneral Motors Mission Statement 2022 | General Motors Mission & Vision Analysis

Date accessed: January 07, 2022 Date published: January 27, 2021.

Chapter 4. Essential # 2 Know their product/service.

1. Article title: Steve Jobs quote #1742229

https://quotepark.com/quotes/1742229-steve-jobs-we-hired-truly-great-people-and-gave-them-the-room/

Website title: Quotepark.com Date accessed: February 25, 2022.

2. 2018 Growth Hiring Trends and research in the US (https://go.sparkhire.com/growth-hiring-trends-united-states-report)

3. Article title: Communicating. Tesla.

https://www.thendobetter.com/investing/2017/9/7/communicating-tesla

Website title: Then Do Better. Date accessed: May 13, 2022. Date published: September 07, 2017.

4. Book title: Emotional intelligence

Book publisher: Bantam Books. Publication year 2020.Page 133.

Chapter 6 Essential # 4 The Mentoring Program. The Art of Building Relationships

1. Article title: Alexander the Great Quote.

https://www.azquotes.com/quote/551168

Website title: A. Date accessed: December 13, 2021.

2. Article title: A quote by Aristotle.

https://www.goodreads.com/quotes/21401-anybody-can-become-angry-that-is-easy-but-to

Website title: Goodreads. Date accessed: February 11, 2022.

3. Article title: A quote by Aristotle

https://www.goodreads.com/quotes/95080-educating-the-mind-without-educating-the-heart-is-no-education

Website title: Goodreads. Date accessed: February 11, 2022.

4. Article title: TOP 25 ARISTOTLE QUOTES ON PHILOSOPHY & VIRTUE: A-Z Quotes

https://www.azquotes.com/author/524-Aristotle

Website title: A. Date accessed: February 05, 2022.

5. Article title: Aristotle.

https://whatsmyquote.com/quote/excellence-or-virtue-is-a-settled-disposition-of-the-mind-that-determines-our-choice-of-actions-and-emotions/page/3

Website title: Aristotle: Excellence or virtue is a settled disposition of the mind t...

Date accessed: February 11, 2022.

6. Article title: Aristotle Quote.

https://quotefancy.com/quote/767784/Aristotle-The-high-minded-man -does-not-bear-grudges-for-it-is-not-the-mark-of-a-great

Website title: Quote fancy. Date accessed: February 11, 2022.

7. Article title: Happy workers are 13% more productive. URL:https://www.ox.ac.uk/news/2019-10-24-happy-workers-are-13-m ore-productive

Website title: University of Oxford. Date accessed: February 04, 2022.

8. Book title: The 21 irrefutable laws of leadership. Book publisher: Thomas Nelson Publishers

Publication year: 1998. Page 130.

9. Article title: Cus D'Amato: the man who met a criminal named Mike Tyson and made him a world champion. URL:https://www.facebook.com/watch/?ref=saved&v=218670915842 832

Website title: Facebook Watch. Date accessed: February 16, 2022. Date published: December 11, 2021.

10. Article title: Cus D'Amato: the man who met a criminal named Mike Tyson and made him a world champion. URL:https://www.facebook.com/watch/?ref=saved&v=218670915842 832

Website title: Facebook Watch. Date accessed: February 16, 2022. Date published. December 11, 2021.

11. Article title: TOP 25 QUOTES BY CUS D'AMATO: A-Z Quotes. https://www.azquotes.com/author/23736-Cus_D_Amato Website title: A

Date accessed: December 15, 2021.

12. Article title: TOP 25 QUOTES BY CUS D'AMATO: A-Z Quotes

https://www.azquotes.com/author/23736-Cus_D_Amato Website title: A

Date accessed: February 05, 2022.

13. Article title: Mike Tyson Training A Younger Version of Himself

https://www.youtube.com/shorts/v-EcL1QciAk Website title: YouTube

Date accessed: May 20, 2022. Date published: April 19, 2022.

14. Article title: A quote by Ronald Reagan. URL

https://www.goodreads.com/quotes/123481-the-greatest-leader-is-not-n ecessarily-the-one-who-does Website title: Goodreads. Date accessed: February 14, 2022.

15. Article title: 45 QUOTES BY ALEXANDER THE GREAT [PAGE - 2]: A-Z Quotes

https://www.azquotes.com/author/5835-Alexander_the_Great?p=2

Website title: A. Date accessed: December 15, 2021.

16. TOP 25 QUOTES BY SIMON SINEK (of 531): A-Z Quotes

https://www.azquotes.com/author/13643-Simon_Sinek

Website title: A. Date accessed: February 10, 2022.

17. Article title: What Is Emotional Intelligence, Daniel Goleman

https://www.ihhp.com/meaning-of-emotional-intelligence/ Website title: IHHP

Date accessed: December 13, 2021. Date published: December 06, 2021.

18. Goleman, Daniel. Emotional Intelligence. (2020. Page xiii.)

Book title: Emotional intelligence. Book publisher: Bantam Books.

Publication year: 2020.

19. Article title: TOP 25 ARISTOTLE QUOTES ON PHILOSOPHY & VIRTUE: A-Z Quotes

https://www.azquotes.com/author/524-Aristotle Website title: A Date accessed:

February 05, 2022

20. Article title: What Makes a Leader? Daniel Goldman. http://www.businessandleadership.com/leadership/item/33518-what-makes-a-leader/

Website title: BUSINESS & LEADERSHIP

Date accessed: December 15, 2021. Date published: November 08, 2021.

Article title: Aristotle Quote: URL: https://www.azquotes.com/quote/814852

Website title: A. Date accessed: July 11, 2022.

22.. https://biblehub.com/niv/proverbs/18.htm

Website title Proverbs 18 NIV. Date accessed: July 11, 2022.

23. https://biblehub.com/isv/1_samuel/1.htm

Website title: 1 Samuel 1 ISV. Date accessed: July 11, 2022.

24. https://biblehub.com/isv/2_kings/4.htm Website title: 2 Kings 4 ISV. Date accessed: July 11, 2022.

25. Author: Goleman, Daniel. Book title: Emotional Intelligence. Book publisher: Bantam Books

Publication year: 2020. Page 137.

26. Article title: A quote from The Art of War

https://www.goodreads.com/quotes/3213455-a-leader-leads-by-example -not-by-force

Website title: Goodreads. Date accessed: February 23, 2022.

27. Book title: Emotional Intelligence. Book publisher: Bantam Books. Publication year: 2020. Page 133.

28. Article title: Cus D'Amato Quote.

https://www.azquotes.com/quote/820049

Website title: A. Date accessed: July 11, 2022.

www.ingramcontent.com/pod-product-compliance
Lightning Source LLC
Chambersburg PA
CBHW062322290526
45794CB00005B/1866